YOUR WORLD

LET'S VISIT A SILVER COMPANY

Billy N. Pope, Ed.D.
South Park Schools,
Beaumont, Texas

Ramona Ware Emmons, M.S.
University of Alabama,
Birmingham, Alabama

ACKNOWLEDGEMENT

We gratefully acknowledge the cooperation and assistance of the personnel and management of the International Silver Company a subsidiary of INSILCO Corporation.

LIBRARY OF CONGRESS CATALOG CARD NO. 79-78295

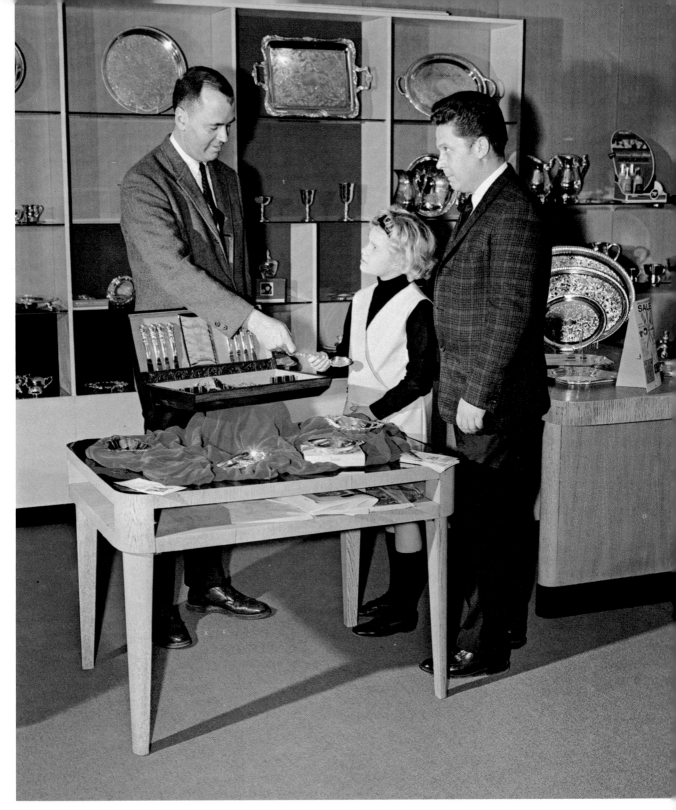

Daddy and I shop at the jewelry store to buy mother a gift. The jeweler shows us a set of silverware.

1735486

We buy the set of silverware for mother. The jeweler makes a bill charging daddy for the silverware. The jeweler makes arrangements for some of my friends and me to visit a silver company.

The president of the silver company welcomes us. He will make arrangements for us to watch silverware being made.

We watch a designer as he makes a new silverware pattern. He is making a model using clay.

Metal dies are made following the pattern made by the designer. The die maker uses a small file to remove small pieces of metal from the pattern. We wear safety glasses in the factory to protect our eyes.

We now visit the rolling mill. We look at the different ingots of metal that will be used to make the silverware.

We watch as the molten metal is poured from the furnace. The different ingots of metal were melted together in the furnace by heat.

This is a furnace used to prepare the metal alloy for rolling. The pieces of metal are called slabs.

We watch the slabs go through the roller. The slabs are flattened by the rollers. The slabs are rolled to certain thicknesses for different kinds of silverware.

We can see our reflections in the slab. The slab is ready to be shipped from the rolling mill to where it will be made into silverware.

This man writes a shipping tag. The slabs have been wrapped in paper and boxed for shipping.

We look at a blank that has been stamped from a large slab. This blank will be made into a fork. Knives, forks, and spoons are called flatware by the silver company.

This lady is cutting spoons. She shows us a blank, the flat spoon, and the piece of metal which is left.

The blank spoons are sent to the machine which will stamp the bowl of the spoon. He shows us the flat spoon and the spoon after it has been stamped.

This is a large striking hammer. The patterns or ornaments are formed on the handles of the fork and spoon by this machine.

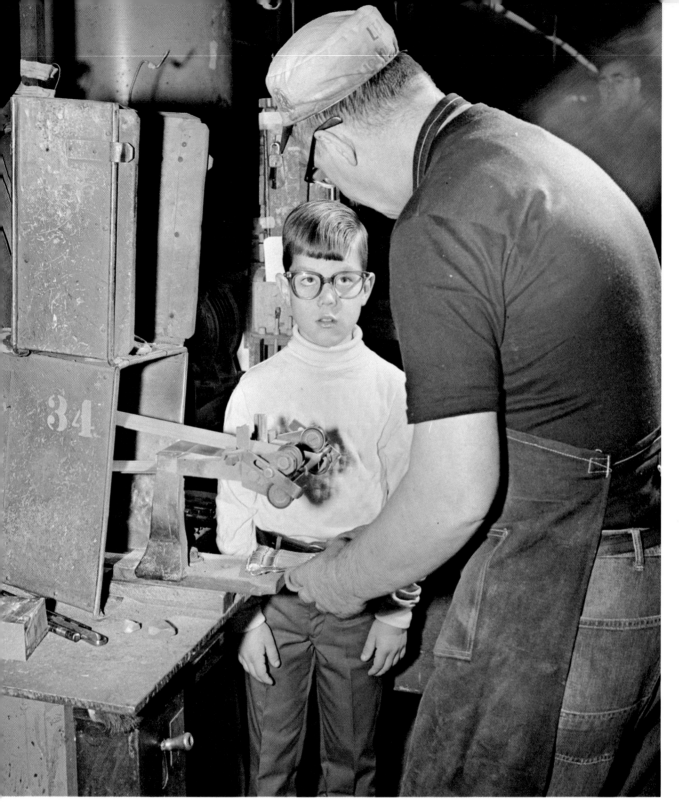

This man uses a belt grinder to remove the rough edges from the spoons after they are stamped with a design.

The spoons are then polished. This worker uses a rack to polish many spoons at one time. A jeweler's rouge is used to polish the pieces of flatware.

The flatware is then washed in hot water with a cleaning solution. This worker uses a rope and pulley to take the tray of spoons from the hot water.

These ladies hang the flatware on racks. The racks will be used to put

the flatware into the silver plating solution.

Electroplating is the process by which the silver is placed on the flat-ware. One worker removes a rack from the solution while another puts a rack into the solution.

We look at the racks of flatware coming from the washer and dryer.
The conveyor carries the racks to where the flatware will be inspected
and packaged.

This woman inspects and packages the pieces of finished flatware. The individual forks are packaged in plastic bags.

We watch a set of spoons being wrapped. The woman carefully inspects each spoon before she wraps the set. She rejects any defective pieces of flatware.

1735486

We look at a complete set of flatware consisting of knives, forks, and spoons being packaged. She also carefully inspects each piece before placing it in the box.

We see the many different patterns which are stored in the stock room. The label on the box shows the name of the silver pattern.

This is the shipping room. The man places the box containing the set of silver in the shipping box. The shipping box will be sent to the jewelry store.

The silversmith presents us a spoon as a souvenir of our visit to the silver company.

Mother opens her gift and is very pleased.

I help mother set the table. She shows me where to place the different pieces of flatware. Would you like to visit a silver company?

LANGUAGE DEVELOPMENT WORDS

A **JEWELRY STORE** has articles made of gold, silver, or precious stones for sale.

A **JEWELER** is one who designs, makes, sells, or repairs jewelry.

SILVERWARE are articles, especially eating and serving utensils, made of silver or silver-plated metals.

A **DESIGNER** is one who devises or executes designs, especially one who creates patterns, as for works of art, dresses, silver, etc.

SILVERWARE PATTERNS are designed by the designers. These patterns range from very fancy and ornate to very plain. Each silverware pattern has a name such as Dubarry.

A flatware **MODEL** is a representation, generally in enlargement, to show the construction or serve as a copy for the flatware pattern.

A **METAL DIE** is made of steel. The steel die is used as an engraved stamp for impressing a design upon some softer material such as silver.

SAFETY GLASSES are glasses made of unbreakable glass for the protection of the eyes. Many industries require employees and visitors to wear safety glasses for protection of their eyes.

A **ROLLING MILL** is a factory where ingots, slabs, or sheets of metal are passed, usually hot, between rolls to give them a certain thickness.

An **INGOT** is a mass of metal cast in a convenient form for shaping, remelting, or refining.

A **METAL ALLOY** is a substance composed of two or more metals mixed as by fusion in a furnace.

A **SLAB** is a semifinished piece of iron, steel, or silver so rolled that its breadth is at least twice its thickness.

A **BLANK** is a piece of metal ready to be drawn, pressed, or machined into a finished object such as a knife, fork, or spoon in a silver company.

FLATWARE is the term given to all implements used in getting the food to the mouth.

JEWELER'S ROUGE or colcothar is the brownish-red oxide or iron used as a polishing agent.

SILVER PLATING is to cover a base metal with silver especially by electroplating.

ELECTROPLATING is to plate or coat with a metal by electrolysis.

CONVEYOR is a mechanical apparatus or machine for carrying flatware from one place to another such as an endless belt, rod, or chain.

INSPECTION is the art of inspecting or viewing to make sure the workmanship is perfect. Imperfect pieces of flatware are returned to the scrap pile.

SILVERSMITH is one whose occupation is making and repairing articles of silver.

Fold line 2

Fold line 1

Place

Time

Date

IT'S A **CELEBRATION** INVITATION

4. Fold on line 2.
5. Color with pens, pencils, paint or crayons.
6. Fill in the blanks inside the card.

INVITATION INSTRUCTIONS

1. Cut off Y and Z.
2. Trim off the remaining three edges of the page.
3. Fold on line 1.

HAVE A HALLELUJAH DAY!

Dropping by to say...

Rejoice in the Lord always. I will say it again: Rejoice! — Philippians 4:4

CARD
INSTRUCTIONS

1. Trim off the outside edge of the page.
2. Fold in half on the solid line.
3. Fold in half again with "Dropping by to say..." on the front and Philippians 4:4 on the back.
4. Color with pens, pencils, paint or crayons.
5. Write a special message inside.

GOD GIVES US RICHLY ALL THINGS TO ENJOY. from 1 Timothy 6:17

THIS IS THE DAY THE LORD HAS MADE;

LET US REJOICE AND BE GLAD IN IT.

Psalm 118:24

INSTRUCTIONS

1. Reproduce bookmarks.
2. Color with markers, pencils, paint or crayons.
3. Glue to cardboard.
4. Optional: Laminate.
5. Cut out.

65

GIANT
BOOKMARK

① Color

② Back with cardboard

③ Cut out

Holy Bible

Let's read about JESUS

REJOICE IN THE LORD ALWAYS

Philippians 4:4

FROM
2 corinthians 9:15

75

FOR GOD

SO LOVED THE WORLD THAT HE SENT JESUS..

From John 3:16

Name

Jesus Loves

☆ Color picture ☆ Add glitter to confetti ☆ Trim off instructions ☆ Hang as series or separately

REJOICE IN THE LORD ALWAYS
Philippians 4:4

REJOICE!

85

YOU WERE GREAT

LET'S CELEBRATE

AWARDED TO

FOR

SIGNED

The joy of the Lord is your strength (Nehemiah 8:10).

Blue Ribbon Award

Presented to

for

by

Date

SHOUT FOR JOY TO THE LORD...
PSALM 100:1

Alphabet...53-61

Balloons..12, 48
Bookmarks...65, 67
Bouncing Party Person.............................17
Bridge..36

Candy...46
Cards..10, 61, 63
Celebration Bridge...................................36
Celebration Invitation...............................61
Certificates.....................................89, 91, 93
Cheesy Popcorn..45
Clothespin Kid...40
Clown..9, 16
Come to the Party...Celebrate Jesus Magnet.............39
Cookies..44
2 Corinthians 9:15...................................75
Creative Salt...45
Cricket...47
Curly Top Treasure Keeper.......................25

Face the Fun...48
Favors...24, 29, 30
Follow Jesus Megaphone............................7
Follow Jesus 3-D Mini Plaque....................23
Follow Me Pendant....................................31

Gift Box Party Favors................................29

Hallelujah Day Card...................................63
Happy Day Potpourri Magnet....................22
Happy/Sad Clown..9
Hat...7
Hip-Hippo-Ray Name Card and Favor.......24
Hip-Hippo-Ray Peekover Room Sign.........26
Hippo Fun..45
Hippo-Partymus Note Holder....................21
Hippo-Partymus Puppet.............................15
Homemade Paint.......................................44
Hot Air Balloon..12

Individual Oatmeal Cookies......................44
Invitations..10, 61

John 3:16..77
Journal...27
Junior Crafts...33

Key chain...39
Kindergarten Crafts....................................5

Lantern..12
"Loggin' For Jesus" Praise Journal............27

Magnets..22, 39
Megaphone..7
Middler Crafts...19

Name Card..6, 24
Napkin Ring...6
Nehemiah 8:10..89
No Bake Peanut Butter Candy..................46
Note Holder...21
Nut Cup Wrapper..6

Oatmeal Cookies.......................................44

Paint..44
Party Accessories..6
Party Alphabet.......................................53-61
Party Favors......................................24, 29,30
Party Hat...7
Party Invitation..10
Party Lantern...12
Party Praise Pom-Pom...............................20
Party Praiser..22
Party Shirts..36
Peanut Butter Candy.................................46
Peekover Room Sign..................................26
Pencils...30
Pendant..31
Philippians 4:4..........................30, 63, 71, 85
Place Card...6, 24
Plaque..23
Pom-Pom...20
Poster Series.............................81, 83, 85
Posters...69-87
Potato Candy...46
Potpourri Magnet......................................22
Praise Journal..27
Preschool Crafts..5
Primary Crafts...19
Psalm 100:1...91
Psalm 118:24..65, 69
Psalm 145:2...73
Pud..45
Puppet...15

Rack...34
Recipes...44,45,46
Room Sign...26

Seashell Party Pals....................................30
"Singin' His Praise" Pencils........................30
Soapsuds Painting......................................44
Stuffed Hot Air Balloon..............................12
Super Surprise Balls..................................44

Tie-Dyed T-Shirts.......................................36
1 Timothy 6:17..65
Treasure Keeper..25
Turnaround Clown.....................................16

Wood Celebration Rack.............................34

Youth Crafts..33

TAKE A BOW

Michael Streff
Illustrator and Designer Extraordinaire

Deonna Lierman
Creator and Coordinator Magnifico

Karen Brewer
Organizer and Rookie Editor

Phyllis Sanders
Director of
Vacation Bible School

Eugene Wigginton
Publisher of
Standard Publishing

Sandy Ziegler
Assistant Director of VBS

Norma Thurman, Editor of
Preschool and Kindergarten Crafts

Margie Redford, Editor of
Primary and Middler Crafts

Cathy Griffith, Editor of
Junior and Youth Crafts

Applause